Helping Organizations

Habitat for Humanity

Anastasia Suen

Rigby

Habitat for Humanity
Copyright © 2001 by Rosen Book Works, Inc.

On Deck™ Reading Libraries
Published by Rigby
a division of Reed Elsevier Inc.
1000 Hart Road
Barrington, IL 60010-2627
www.rigby.com

Book Design: Michelle Innes
Text: Anastasia Suen
Photo Credits: Cover, pp. 5–7, p. 8 (bottom), pp. 9–13, 15–20
© Habitat for Humanity; p. 8 (top) © Corbis

06 05 04 03 02 01
10 9 8 7 6 5 4 3 2 1

Printed in The United States of America

ISBN 0-7635-7874-6

Contents

Millard and Linda Fuller

Millard and Linda Fuller wanted to help people all over the world build their own homes. In 1976, the Fullers began Habitat for Humanity International. Habitat for Humanity International works to make sure that everyone has a good place to live.

Volunteers

Many people help Habitat for Humanity. They work as volunteers.

Some people help build or fix houses. Others give money or supplies to Habitat for Humanity.

In 1984, former U.S. President Jimmy Carter and his wife, Rosalynn, joined Habitat for Humanity. They wanted to help people build their own homes, too.

Jimmy Carter was the 39th president of the United States (1977–1981).

Jimmy Carter helped build the 100,000th house for Habitat for Humanity in 2000.

The Carters started the Jimmy Carter Work Project. Volunteers build homes for Habitat for Humanity for one week each year. People come from all over the United States to help.

It's a Fact

In one week, the Jimmy Carter Work Project built more than 100 homes!

Many students help to build houses. Every year, students from ages 5 to 25 volunteer in the United States. Some even go to other countries to help.

Helping Around the World

Habitat for Humanity has built homes all over the world. More than half of the homes built each year are outside the United States.

It's a Fact

Habitat for Humanity works in more than 70 countries worldwide.

Habitat for Humanity at Work

Volunteers work together to build a home in New Zealand.

Habitat for Humanity builds many different kinds of houses. Houses in Papua New Guinea are built on stilts.

This house in Sri Lanka was made with concrete. Concrete houses are very strong. Habitat houses all over the world have survived earthquakes, floods, and hurricanes!

New Homeowners

Habitat for Humanity houses aren't free. The people who will live in the houses must help to build them. They also have to pay for the materials that are used. In the United States, the materials for one Habitat for Humanity house cost about $46,000.

Since 1976, Habitat for Humanity has grown. It has built and fixed more than 100,000 homes around the world. More than 500,000 people live in better homes thanks to Habitat for Humanity International.

It's a Fact

A Habitat for Humanity team from New Zealand built a house in 3 hours, 44 minutes, and 59 seconds!

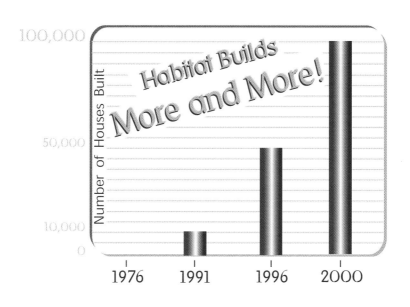

Habitat Builds More and More!

Number of Houses Built

100,000

50,000

10,000

0

1976   1991   1996   2000

Glossary

habitat (**hab**-uh-tat) the place where someone lives

humanity (hyoo-**man**-uh-tee) all human beings

international (ihn-tuhr-**nash**-uh-nuhl) having to do with two or more countries

materials (muh-**tihr**-ee-uhlz) what things are made of

Papua New Guinea (**pa**-pooh-a **noo gihn**-ee) a country in the southwestern Pacific Ocean

Sri Lanka (**sree lang**-kuh) an island country in the Indian Ocean

stilts (**stihlts**) strong poles that are used to raise a house above the ground

volunteers (vahl-uhn-**tihrz**) people who work without pay

Resources

Books

The Big Help Book: 365 Ways You Can Make a Difference by Volunteering
by Alan Goodman
Minstrel Books (1994)

The Kids' Volunteering Book
by Arlene Erlbach
Lerner Publications (1998)

Web Site

Habitat for Humanity International
http://www.habitat.org

Index